What's Inside Lakes?

Jane Kelly Kosek

The Rosen Publishing Group's
PowerKids Press™
New York

For Mom and Dad—two wonderful parents who have enjoyed countless hours on the Great Lakes. Thanks for your support.

Published in 1999 by The Rosen Publishing Group, Inc.
29 East 21st Street, New York, NY 10010

First Edition

Book Design: Kim Sonsky

Photo Credits: Cover, title page, contents, pp. 14, 17 © 1996 PhotoDisc; p. 5 © International Stock/Mark Newman; p. 6 © FPG/Don Herbert; p. 8 © 1997 Digital Vision Ltd.; pp. 9, 16 © FPG/Gail Shumway; p. 10 © International Stock/NASA; p. 13 © FPG/Shinichi Kanno; p. 18 © International Stock/Bob Firth; p. 21 © FPG/David Sacks.

Kosek, Jane Kelly.
    What's inside lakes? / by Jane Kelly Kosek.
        p.   cm. — (The what's inside library)
    Includes index.
    Summary: Discusses how different types of lakes are formed, the creatures that live in lakes, such as fish, snails, algae, and otters, and explains how they survive.
    ISBN 0-8239-5280-0
    1. Lake ecology—Juvenile literature. 2. Lakes—Juvenile literature. [1. Lake ecology. 2. Ecology. 3. Lakes.] I. Title. II. Series: Kosek, Jane Kelly. What's inside library.
QH541.5.L3K67 1998
577.63—dc21   98-15981
                                                                                      CIP
                                                                                       AC

Manufactured in the United States of America

Contents

What Are Lakes?

Lakes are large areas of freshwater or salt water. Lakes are important because they store water when there is a large amount of rainfall. Then this water can be used when there is less rainfall.

Lakes also help to **regulate** (REG-yoo-layt) the flow of rivers by slowly releasing their stored water into the rivers. Larger lakes are sometimes called seas. The world's largest lake is the Caspian Sea. It is about 760 miles across and lies between Asia and Europe. The world's deepest lake is Lake Baikal in Russia. It has a **depth** (DEPTH) of 5,314 feet. About half of the lakes on our entire planet Earth are in Canada.

Lake Baikal is 50 miles wide and over 300 miles long. ▶

How Do Lakes Form?

Lakes form in many ways. Most lakes, including the Great Lakes in the United States and Canada, are in **hollows** (HOL-ohz) that were made by **glaciers** (GLAY-sherz) thousands of years ago. During a time in history called the Ice Age, huge glaciers covered large areas of land. As Earth warmed up in some of these areas, the glaciers moved and melted, leaving many hollows. The rain, melted ice, and snow that fell into these hollows formed lakes. Some lakes, such as Lake Victoria in East Africa, are found in cracks in Earth's crust. Others are in **volcanoes** (vol-KAY-nohz) that are no longer active. A lake may form from a section of a river that has been cut off from the rest of that river. Lakes are also formed by people or beavers, usually by **damming** (DAM-ing) a creek or river.

◀ Some lakes, such as this one in Costa Rica, form in volcano craters.

How Do Lakes Get Their Water?

Why don't lakes just dry up? Some do if they lose water faster than they gain it. The **water cycle** (WAH-ter SY-kul) is what helps lakes stay full. To describe the water cycle, let's start with the water in the ocean. Each day the sun's heat causes water from the ocean to **evaporate** (ee-VAP-er-ayt) and rise as water vapor. Water vapor forms the clouds we see in the sky. Next, the water in the clouds falls back to Earth as rain or snow. As the rain or snow hits land, it may run off quickly into lakes, streams, or the ocean. Or it may make its way slowly through the ground to these bodies of water. Eventually, the water that started in the ocean makes its way back to the ocean. Then the cycle starts again.

Earth's water cycle is important to all creatures. ▶

Lake Superior

Lake Huron

Lake
Michigan

Freshwater Lakes

The Great Lakes form the largest body of freshwater in the world. They include Lake Erie, Lake Huron, Lake Michigan, Lake Ontario, and Lake Superior. Freshwater is very important to living things. Some of our drinking water comes from freshwater lakes. Freshwater is less **dense** (DENS) than salt water. This is because it does not contain as much **matter** (MAT-er) as saltwater lakes. More kinds of plants and animals can live in freshwater because it can hold more **oxygen** (AHK-sih-jin) and has less salt than salt water. Plants and animals need oxygen to live.

◄ The Great Lakes are so large they can be seen clearly from space.

Saltwater Lakes

A saltwater lake can be almost as salty or even saltier than the ocean. The saltiest lake in the world is the Dead Sea, which is ten times saltier than the ocean. There is so much salt in the Dead Sea that **columns** (KOL-umz) of salt stick out of the water. A lake can become salty if its water evaporates faster than it is replaced.

Saltwater lakes have very little oxygen. This means that these lakes do not have as many plants and animals living in them as in freshwater lakes. For example, the Dead Sea only has **algae** (AL-jee) and **bacteria** (bak-TEER-ee-uh) living in it.

The Dead Sea is so dense with salt that it does not create waves and it's impossible to sink in it. ▶

Life in a Lake

There are three main areas in a lake where life is usually found. These include shallow water areas, the open water, and the bottom of the lake. Different kinds of things live in each area. Plants live only in areas where sunlight can reach them. They need sunlight for **energy** (EN-er-jee), which helps them grow. Most plants grow in shallow water areas. Since plants release oxygen into the water, most of the other living things in a lake live near them. Some creatures are able to live on the bottom of the lake. They eat plants or dead animals that float down from above.

◀ The plants and animals that live around and in a lake, such as this duck and these water plants, learn to live together and depend on each other.

What Lives in a Lake?

Plants such as algae and other water plants can live in a lake. You may also find animals such as crayfish, snails, or shrimp. Many different kinds of fish live in lakes, such as bass, perch, pike, sunfish, or trout. Some **mammals** (MA-mulz) live in lakes, including otters and seals. You may even find snakes in a lake. All of these animals' bodies are made to live in water. But plants and animals may be different from lake to lake. For example, the only freshwater seal in the world lives in Russia's Lake Baikal.

Crayfish (left) and otters (right) are just two examples of very different ▶ animals that may share a lake as their home.

Under a Frozen Lake

During the winter, many lakes freeze. A lake freezes from its surface down. However, even the coldest winter usually does not freeze a lake all the way through. When a lake is not completely frozen, water still exists underneath a layer of ice. As long as the water under the ice contains enough oxygen, you can still see living things under the ice. During the winter, when the ice is safe enough to walk across, some people even cut holes in the thick ice and go fishing.

◄ Walking or fishing on a frozen lake can be fun, but first the ice must be thick enough to support people.

Pollution

Have you ever seen a sign near a lake that says: *DANGER: NO SWIMMING OR FISHING*? The lake might be too **polluted** (puh-LOO-ted) to swim or fish in. Some lakes are polluted with **sewage** (SOO-ij), which is dumped by people. Lakes may also be polluted with **pesticides** (PES-tih-sydz) and **fertilizers** (FER-tih-ly-zerz) from farms. This pollution can cause a lake to become **eutrophic** (yoo-TROH-fik). A eutrophic lake uses up its oxygen faster than it can produce it. Without oxygen, everything in the lake may die. But polluted lakes can be saved if people try to clean them up.

Because of pollution, lakes that were once fun for swimming and fishing in are now so dirty they can't be used. ▶

20

Caring for Our Lakes

We depend on lakes for many things. They give us water to drink, plants and fish to eat, and places to fish and swim. But today many lakes are polluted or are losing large amounts of water.

People are learning how to take care of our lakes so we don't lose them. You can help by **recycling** (ree-SY-kling) your trash and using less water. Turn off the water while you're brushing your teeth. And make sure there are no dripping faucets in your home. By doing these things, you are helping our lakes live longer!

Web Sites:

You can find out more about lakes at these Web sites:
http://www.great - lakes.net/
http://www.mobot.org/MBGnet/fresh/lakes/

Glossary

algae (AL-jee) A plant without roots or stems that usually lives in water.

bacteria (bak-TEER-ee-uh) A very small living thing.

column (KOL-um) A tall, thin structure.

damming (DAM-ing) To hold back water to form a pond or lake.

dense (DENS) Thick.

depth (DEPTH) How deep something is.

energy (EN-er-jee) A force in nature that makes activity.

eutrophic (yoo-TROH-fik) When too many nutrients in a lake use up all of the oxygen and the lake eventually dies.

evaporate (ee-VAP-er-ayt) To change from a liquid to a gas.

fertilizer (FER-tih-ly-zer) A human-made substance that helps crops grow.

glacier (GLAY-sher) A large body of ice covering part of the earth.

hollow (HOL-oh) A hole in the ground.

mammal (MA-mul) An animal that has a backbone and breathes air. It also gives birth to live young and feeds its babies milk from its body.

matter (MAT-er) The material that makes up something.

oxygen (AHK-sih-jin) A colorless gas that many forms of life need to live.

pesticide (PES-tih-syd) A human-made substance that is used to kill insects.

polluted (puh-LOO-ted) When an area is filled with garbage and waste.

recycle (ree-SY-kul) To reuse.

regulate (REG-yoo-layt) To control the speed of something.

sewage (SOO-ij) Waste.

volcano (vol-KAY-noh) An opening in Earth's crust through which hot, liquid rock is sometimes forced out.

water cycle (WAH-ter SY-kul) The process by which water evaporates from bodies of water and then returns to them as rain or snow.

Index